Resurrection Biology

ACKNOWLEDGMENTS

The author would like to thank the publications in which the following poems appeared
(sometimes in earlier versions).

Atticus Review: "Cosmic Background Radiation"
Barefoot Review: "Speechless" and "Hijacked"
Best American Poetry Blog: "Do a Little, Make a Little…"
Blueline: "The Visitors"
DMQ: "Etymology"
Dos Passos Review: "Bald"
The Enchanting Verses: "Interstice" and "The Feathered Man"
MIPOesias: "Dream of Two Bears"
OCHO: "Letter from Guantanamo," "August Pastoral," and "Relocation"
Omega : "The Boy in the Snow"
Poets Against War Online: "Salvage and Rescue" and "In September"
The Poets' Cookbook: German and American Cooking: ""Sister Parsnip"
Zocalo Public Square: "Resurrection Biology," "Hibernation, Ursa Major" (as "Ursa
Major"), and "The Last Widow"

"Castrata: a Conversation" was published as a chapbook by Finishing Line Press, 2014.

"Hibernation: Ursa Major" has been adapted as part of the song cycle *The Constellations* by
Michael Thaxton.

Deepest gratitude and love to Anne Caston, Grace Cavalieri, Norma Conner, Stacey
Harwood, Leslie McGrath, Jill Alexander Essbaum Peng, and Maria Van Beuren.

Publisher: Leah Maines
Editor: Christen Kincaid
Cover Art: "Passenger Pigeons" by Lewis Cross, 1900. Image in public domain;
          painting in the Grand Rapids Art Museum. Photo by Ethan Beute.
Author Photo: Richard Orem
Cover Design: Elizabeth Maines

Printed in the USA on acid-free paper.
Order online: www.finishinglinepress.com
          also available on amazon.com

Author inquiries and mail orders:
Finishing Line Press
P. O. Box 1626
Georgetown, Kentucky 40324
U. S. A.

Table of Contents

I

II

III

For Rick

I

"Do a Little, Make a Little..."

If we didn't know who we were, we knew
we wanted to dance.
                    Here, a world made
of light and color, music and movement,
a casino of the imagination where the wheel
always came up red. The songs were mindless
but pulsed a rhythm like sex, like breaking away
toward something else—we weren't sure what,
but we ached to go there.
                    Such clichés now, decades on,
but we threw the artificial stars from mirrored globes
across our shoulders and boogied down on electric floors—
do a little dance, make a little love, get down tonight.
We drank cheap lambrusco with 7-Up, sloe gin fizzes,
and gave the bartender our tiny purses to keep safe
while we prowled the room—girls made up
like baby drag queens, all hairspray, glitter, and slick
lipgloss, checking out boys who dripped fake gold chains
from their bare, skinny chests—
How many polyesters did you kill to make that suit?
The foxiest girls slipped outside
to sniff cocaine from tiny silver spoons
in the backseats of candy-colored muscle cars.
We coveted their feathered hair and perfect skin,
their grace on platform shoes, the way
the beautiful boys took their hands and
led them out the door.
When we hit the dance floor,
we sang along as if we knew real loss—
I will survive—as long as I know how to love, I know I'll stay alive—
waiting for that thing to happen
that would make all of this, whatever
it was, come true.

Salvage and Rescue

*"You can tell a true war story by its absolute and
uncompromising allegiance to obscenity and evil."*
—Tim O'Brien

In my father's stories, the most terrible thing
was the death of Lady, a fluffy white dog
so small she could fit in the pocket
of a sailor's peacoat—the ship's mascot,
washed overboard in a storm.

But most days the Caribbean was a blue jewel
set with the green jewels of Haiti, Cuba, Trinidad.
The Andrews Sisters drank rum and Coca-Cola,
dolphins leapt at the tumblehome,
and off the coast of Venezuela, magic—
a thousand parrots appeared
one morning perched in the rigging.
As the sailors drank their coffee,
the birds arced a moveable rainbow
across the brightening sky.

In my father's stories, adventure was dodging
the skipper's pet monkey,
a nimble-fingered thief who'd steal
a man's glasses right off his nose
and chatter maniacally from the top
of the crow's nest, just out of reach.

And in my father's stories, no one ever wept
with loneliness when no letter from home
arrived at mail call. No one imagined his children
growing up as strangers. No one crouched
under the shadow of the big guns on the bow,
gibbering a panicked prayer
that the shell hit anyone else but him
No one begged, *Let me live, let me live.*
No one killed an enemy—
no enemies to be found

in my father's stories. No U-boats dodged
depth charges to spit evil-eyed torpedoes
at Allied convoys. No ship sank,
no sailor swam in desperate slow motion
away from the flaming hulk, suction pulling
irresistibly at his heel. No pleading survivors
were machine-gunned in their lifeboats.

In his stories, my father never hauled
over the ship's rail a half-drowned man
burned black with gasoline, puking salt water
and blood and diesel fuel across the fantail,
never pulled a dead man from the ocean,
bloated from floating days and days
in the tropical sun, never cursed as the man burst
his stinking innards onto the steel-plated deck.
He never checked a dog tag, thumbed a wallet,
compared the swollen tongue, the jutting
bones, the eyeholes black as marbles
with a sodden ID card or dissolving snapshot,

never wrote a letter to
a friend's widow and children
to tuck in the box of personal belongings.
My father never trembled sleepless in his bunk,
waiting for the blare of general quarters,
the whistle of a bomb dropped
from a thousand feet up,
or just the flash and blast, then
the cold, terrible sea.

In September

The stars hang alone in the late-summer sky,
empty for the first time in a hundred years.
So still, not even the barest breath
of wind ruffles the dog's fur.

Once upon a time, the growl of an airplane
called the whole town into the street,
pointing and marveling
at the wonderful new machine.

We are hunkered down, waiting,
but the dog still needs her walk.
In the clear archaic night, we can see light
years beyond each celestial body—
Didn't Einstein say the universe curves
back to its beginning? Maybe if we look deep enough
we will see ourselves looking deep
at ourselves.
Or maybe vision just dissolves
in the unknowable dark. Maybe all we see
is nighttime, after all.

In the whirling universe, the world hasn't moved an inch.
The dog pokes her snout into the grass,
wags her tail, moves on.
There's nothing new here she can smell.

Even the stars know that.
No need to look up and tell them so.

Hibernation, Second Winter

The air goes crisp and sharp
as a Mackintosh apple or
the sound of a rifle
in the woods.

Then she knows
to seek out hidden places
under roots or rockpiles,
deeper, more secret
than the cold.

Sleepy-eyed, torpid,
she lumbers in, hunches
the dark around her shoulders
like another coat or
mossy camouflage
to hide her for a frozen
time.

      She dreams
a season long
of nuts and berries, trees
and flowered meadow grass
bending in warm breezes,
the good green spring
to wake her later on.

The Boy in the Snow

All night you lay there
bleeding until an early morning
commuter spied you and called
the cops. You were still

alive when they got there,
despite two stab wounds
to the chest, despite the chill
of the snowbank you wrapped

yourself around for hours.
They had no idea who you were.
No one had reported you
missing or truant or run away.

You were fourteen. You sprawled
black against white turning pink, turning
red, a knit cap askew on your head,
baggy jeans twisted around your hips,

diffused by their silent, interior elegy
that a boy like you, alone
at night, with no one
to miss you, got what he deserved.

Through a gate of trees beyond
your body, the cops could see
the lights of houses so close
they might have heard you

shout, if you had time to shout.

Speechless

All my language falls amiss.
Illness amputates the tongue.
There is no metaphor for this.

It empties every word, insists
on facts, each ugly one.
There is no metaphor for this.

I'm stupid as stone, a useless
sheep, and just as dumb.
All my language goes amiss,

consumed by suffering's avarice.
I'd say *the world's no longer young*
but there's no metaphor for this

that won't go up in a smoky hiss,
sleet upon a fire's prong.
All of language falls amiss,

and echoes blank, ridiculous.
Each sinew of the heart's unstrung.
See? All my language gone amiss.
There is no metaphor for this.

Hijacked

The summer has been hijacked—
not by a knife-wielding crazy who wants
to crash in a blaze of jihadist glory,
but by ill-health, the disease
that gives license for lurid tales
of how grandmothers died of the same thing,
mothers, aunts, sisters who were only thirty and left
three small children.

Not that that will happen to you

they are quick to say, as if that erases
the vivid detail of the kind of misery
you might face,
                "They Mean Well"
a billboard on this road to hell
that you will do your best to bail off
long before it actually goes anywhere.

It could be worse.

It could be so much worse

you repeat like a Buddhist koan.
You have that precious ticket so many don't,
the way out, access to the exit
ramp that leads back
to what is normal. You look
at the ticket to remind yourself
by fall the chemo will be over,
that your life will again belong to you,
that you will live.

This is something.

No, it is everything,

but still this summer is a lost season,
the birdsong minored
by suffering and illness, even the colors
of the flowers slightly off, as if
they too are feeling it deep in their roots
where the damage is invisible and does not heal.

Fire at the Back

Is it better to jump
than to burn?
The Triangle girls, broken
on the sodden pavement—
are they easier to bear
than their sisters seared
into namelessness
on the melted workroom floor?

And the falling man
plummeting 100 stories but fixed
in space—what hope
do we wrench
from the frozen smoke
mirrored his shoes?

Look again! His smoldering shirt
billows cotton wings.
He is a seagull, lifted
on sunlit thermals, not falling,
but flying.

Letter from Guantanamo

Seasons don't matter except
for the discomfort they bring.
June is just hotter.

The Caribbean thuds against Cuba,
steaming like soup, saltier
than our tears,
if anyone cried here.

Whether we bear it or not,
the pain continues.

The interrogator takes his work
as seriously as Michelangelo
considered the perfect pink
of God's fingertips.

Once I ate sweet dates and dreamed
of doing something important.

Now the sun, that holy eye,
stares down on the sea and sand,
strikes us blind.

Gaza Beach

for Ismail, Ahed, Zakariya, and Mohammed Bakir

And how could you know
the big gun's laser eye
had trapped you from the sea,
burned targets into your backs,
oh little brown boys,
little footballers, little symbols
of something not to be borne,
how could you know
that sunlight impaled you dark
against the sugar-white beach,
how could you know
that hate would eat you
like breakfast and drool
your blood across the sand?

Radium Girls

We make time luminesce,
our numbers bright as moonglow.

Precise work, oh yes—we lick the brush sharp
after three, after six, then nine, then twelve.

Our quotas absorb us, hunched over the table
ten hours a day, until six o'clock Friday

unlocks us like a key from our benches,
and we are girls again. We splash giddy

magic on our fingertips and hair,
trace brilliant strokes across our eyelids

to dazzle sweet boys on Saturday night.
Such pretty pixies, how we sparkle and dance!

In unseen places, we are cracking and crumbling.
Our bones shatter and burn.

The Bears of Abruzzo

Thirty white stones on a green hill,
green to the sea smudging blue into sky.

Thirty brown bears upend
the stones to see
what's beneath—the hidden prize
of grub and bug, perpetual
antipasto to munch on all day.
The stones are blocks, are boulders,
but with muscled ease
they flip them like pebbles
on a rocky beach.

Scholarly Hadrian sought them
in hundreds, in thousands—
ursae validos, orsi forti—
as if in the blood they spilled
their strength became his own.

Oblivious as landscape
they tread the craggy tor on claws
now meant for digging, not
orchestrated battle.

What do we abandon and what
do we hold? What holds to us,
a rope to pull the splintered
wreck to shore?

Thirty brown bears move
cold white stones across
the hillside tumbling green
to the sea, then sleep in Abruzzo.
Only thirty. No more.

Etymology

1.   *Portage*

First the earthquake tore
    the Alaskan ground, spitting
        out the shoreline six feet down in half
            a minute.

Next the great wave swept
    the houses from stone to shingle,
        drowning the mountains
            a thousand feet up.

For a time landscape
    was ocean floor.
        Then the water rushed out
            Turnagain Arm to the proper sea

leaving just one crippled tilting house
    and a rim of skeleton pines,
        their groping roots awash in salty poison.

2.   *portal*

When the Alutiiq saw the whale,
breeching in bone-cold water,
it was
    ar'uq

the door to understanding one word wide.

Through it

blubber blowhole baleen
fins tail the blood-red meat

sacred spirit of essential whale

In naming, perception—
So we believe, and swallow
dictionaries whole like medicine,
scour the Web for definitions
and wait to know the thing, as if
vocabulary and syntax
forge keys into insight.

Look   listen

here I have words,

>   *adenocarcinoma, neuroendocrine differentiation*

but this language, my language

>   *neoplasm, carboplatin, taxotere*

curves its clinical tendrils round the frame
but cannot unlock the why, the what next, the will I

Like a stone into the sea
it disappears within the murky green
and finds the secret place
where terror sounds the astounding deep.

3.   *port*

Two cuts to place the metal
disk, stitched down tight
into my breastbone. An opening,
a secret known only

to initiates, its password spell
a Latinate cantation
to ward off the evil eye.

Two snaky tongues feed
their venom through the larger vessels,
light chemical backfires
                    burning burning burning
no tidal wave can quench.

Two nurses, gowned and masked, float
near and then away, then near again
like blue paper lanterns on an unseen current.
The TV's drone cannot drown out
the simplest of facts: You must

let in the beast to kill the beast.

My mouth corrodes like rusted metal.
Timor mortis conturbat me.
Don't come in. Come in.

4.   *portage*

Even now there is no easy passage, no
fathoms-deep canal carved
to let the gravid oil tankers through.
Even now, the only way is over.

A thousand generations of footsteps
imprinted on this beach,
where the first Alutiiq
hauled ashore their boats of bark and skin,
strapped them tight across their shoulders

to navigate a route to
more distant water.

That night they watched
the sparking embers of their fire fall back
hissing in the frigid snowmelt.
They wondered when they would find
the sea, when what they carried
would carry them again.

Bald

Remember, remember that boy
who could not love you
because you were not pretty,
whose terrible honesty you've carried
these years, the truth you mined from him
like some strange gemstone made of your
own desperation that you still wear
around your neck.

And now this boy, your boy, who carefully wields
the electric razor until, stroke by stroke,
your head is shaven, austere as a nun's,
beauty or lack of it irrelevant as it is to God. This is
about power. This is about mess. This is what you do
to claim some purchase on this absurd slide
down a hill of talus looking for meaning
or Jesus or some way to make sense.
The boy reminds you as he shifts
to a disposable razor and, surgically careful,
scrapes away the tiniest stubble, black and gray
as a prophet's beard. *Your choice,* he says. My choice,
like forcing truth from another boy years ago.
See, says my son. *Look. It's not so bad.*
You can stand it. You already have.
Stand it some more.

II

Castrata: a Conversation

"What is the body? Rain on a window,
A clear movement over whose gaze?
Husk, leaf, little boat of paper

and wood to mark the speed of the stream?"

—*Mark Doty, "Atlantis"*

1.

My body turned upon itself and burst,
but with their flashing knives the doctors staved
the rushing flood. Left behind a grave
wound, but see, I lived to tell the tale first
hand. Gratitude is stamped across my head.
I'm grateful as a pruned tree, an engine
with new plugs, Rover with a juicy bone.
After all, I didn't end up dead.
(Now, take a deep breath. Smile and don't rehash
the bloody scenes.) One and two and three
and through, just like that, and all was swell.
The fix was in. Or would be with a dash
of chemistry. The woman who used to be me
burnt away to ash and smoke, who could tell?

2. Farinelli is Operated Upon

They burned away, with ash and smoke to tell
them when the fix was in. My crystal voice
secured, their fortune, too. Don't cry. A choice
made above my head, it's true, but I will
thank them one day, when I sing for the king.
Manhood's a small price to pay for your song,
an angelic marvel of breath and tone.
Little one, you'll be rich as anything
your shabby family can dare to dream.
Don't cry. The fix is in. What they would give
for art, I've already given. I fill
my heart with that, although it may still seem
the blood and pain were worth—Nothing? Well, grief
can be its own kind of art, if you will.

3. *Farinelli Speaks of Grief*

Grief is its own kind of art, if you will.
But what it conjures in us is unseen,
like cancer dark inside a body, screened
against the prurient eye. Don't kill
the reader when he can't see the poem
or hear the song or quite yet understand
what it is he's entitled to demand
of what we've hidden here. Leave him alone.
We're liars. We pretend we're whole, complete
as jigsaw puzzles in their boxes, no
missing parts explained. We have rehearsed
our competence to a T. We will meet
the world with painted scrims as faces, though
we can't pretend away our raging thirst.

4.

I can't pretend away my rage, a thirst
that can't be quenched even by prognosis
excellent. (I could be dead. I know this.)
I remember the body I wore, all lust
and hunger and strength and prowling and lithe
appetite—now I'm dried and brittle as
old sticks and matches, something as little as
one measly cinder could burn me alive.
Oh, yes, this is the stuff of poetry:
The hallway leads into an empty house,
a place of echoes, fixtures ripped away,
vacant, a delicious old irony
of a house, an architect's futile cause.
I write all this, then throw it all away.

5.

I write all this, then toss it all away:
I'm going to die someday. Everyone says
they know, but just like sex or Vietnam,
you have to have been there, and so I was.
But so what? I know a woman, as calm
as toast, who ticks a box off every day
like bonus points won in three-card-monte.
Her calendar's improbable X's
encroach each month like the incoming tide.
She should be dead. She's not. No one suspects.
So why do I complain and whine and grind
my teeth? I'll put on some Belafonte
and pour a drink, and act my age with grace,
show off my glittering poetry face.

6. *Farinelli Speaks of Art*

Show off like glittering poetry. Face
the crowd with arrogant elegance
because you know the sound you make will dance
into the rafters, make the ladies unlace
their bodices, fall backwards in a faint
of ecstasy. There's no music like mine.
The resonant O, the clarion chime,
those purest of notes pluck the hearts of saints
and not-so-saintly both. I'm drowning in lace
hankies and money and offers of love
from women too silly to know what it
means to be me. But it's something. Though not
what I would have, I'll still take it. Above
us my song, ghostly bell to haunt this place.

7. Farinelli Speaks of Love

My ghostly bell, once heard, haunts every place,
stage and boudoir, dawn and dusk and dream.
It brings me wealth and fame. A kind of sex,
too, but not love, no. The sort of embrace
that pleases them but leaves me as I seem:
aloof, alone, one of love's architects
but not in residence. Single by law,
why would I love? Nothing could come of it.
Truth is, it's all right. I drink in applause
like good wine, count my money and plaudits
in the press. *Orpheus had not a voice
like his*, they say: riches to stash away.
And what else could I do? What other choice
is there for me? I can't change night to day.

8.

I've got sense. I can't change night to day,
of course. I live "in the now," as TV shrinks
repeat. But see, here is the present now:
a body gone to hell, teeth that break, gray-
ing of everything. The bluest day stinks
of mortality. Like an ancient cow,
I trundle from bed to table to desk,
gumming my cud and remembering when
I frisked for all the bulls. But as they say,
the fix is in: Still alive, and grotesques
have their panache, a currency to spend.
That is, if seen. I shimmer between rays
of sunlight and shadow-blackened air.
I think at fifty women disappear.

9.

I think at fifty women disappear,
turn ghostly mist, like fog or smoke at dusk.
Vaporous beings, no outline there,
the throb and juice and tang of thirty's musk
gone flat like morning's tepid Pepsi in
a glass left out at bedtime. That's a joke,
but even the bagboys don't take you in
at the grocery store. You have to speak,
then they look up, surprised.
                              What matters cancer
then? A body's rusted, keyless lock?
I've had my run. Once is better than none
at all. But still: I want, I want—the knock,
the pulse and blood, the flicker of fire.
I still want. The she inside won't expire.

10.

I still want. The she inside won't expire
like quarts of milk or ancient cans of beans.
Souls are more than broken bodies. Enquire
within for the sexual id. Hot dreams
not needed or asked for. If you hand me
a cactus, I want a daisy. A poem,
I want a cabbage root, a rose, a tree
or fern. I am never happy, Handsome.
I eat discontent. But if I'm alive,
well, then I'm alive, with all of the mess
and the slap and the push of the living.
Hold nothing back—even kisses arrive
like a sacrament, carnal eucharist
of the damned. I want. I want. I'm raving.

11. *Farinelli Goes to Spain*

The damned still want. You can hear them raving
above hell's deep roar of cheers and applause.
I took the offer, went to Spain to sing,
antidote for the melancholic king:
a frozen monarch in misery's maw
who dreamed my music would rush like a spring
over his sadness. Oh, he paid me well
enough to stand each night and go through my
repertoire. But soon it was more than this:
I magicked him. My voice conjured a spell
of physick, or prayer. At once his bleared eye
awoke; sometimes he smiled, a look like bliss.
From madness I saved him, year after year.
What is a man's mind worth? How much despair

12. *Farinelli Weighs It Up*

is his mind, whole, worth? Equate my despair
and my grief to his restored sanity—
What comes the balance then? Are they the same
in value and in pain? If we'd be fair,
tell me who suffers more: a fat wealthy
singer, or a man who eats of his shame
each day as he wishes to die? Would I
invert things, get back all that was taken,
give back what I got, including his mind?
Yet the other side, weighted with loneli-
ness, is heavy. To love and awaken
to being loved—to imagine that kind
of common joy is playing with fire:
Art and goodness—both corrode from desire.

13.

Is all that's good corroded by desire?
On the one hand, wisdom and poems and life.
But on the other, all that I have lost
dangles its absence in front of me, fruit
going rotten on its vine. A brutal
joke, it just bobs there in the air, the cost
of survival. If you'd stood with the knife
over me, said *choose*, I'd be a liar
if I claimed I would have said no. Of course
life is the thing that matters, yes. Yet
these haunt me, too: delicious cravings
of sex, strength of limb, the relentless force
inhabiting the self. I hedged my bet.
Here's the price: the body that I'm grieving.

14.

The price for life: the body I'm grieving.
That's fair enough. It's good to be alive,
not decomposing like last year's old mulch.
The fix is in. I eat and I'm breathing,
fingers and toes accounted for. Believe
me, there is joy in a traceable pulse.
If illness is a crucible, I'm poured
and forged, hot-molded into something new,
annealed. But I will name my losses, too:
a body rampant, that sweetness, soured
by knowledge that a season has been cursed
and burned and can't be gotten back again.
No use to pretend it didn't happen:
My body turned upon itself and burst.

15.

My body turned upon itself and burst,
then burnt away, ashes, smoke, who could tell?
But grief's its own kind of art, if you will:
I can't pretend away my rage, my thirst
to write all this. But I toss it away,
show off my glittering poetry face,
a ghost ringing bells in a haunted place
as if she could change the night into day.
I think at fifty women disappear—
Still, the she inside never expires.
The damned want and want, and go on raving.
And what's she worth? How much despair?
Is all that's good corroded by desire?
The price for life: the body I'm grieving.

III

Resurrection Biology

Bring out the dead—the passenger
pigeon and Carolina parakeet,
the Tasmanian tiger, the dodo,
the mammoth still sleeping
in icy Neolithic dreams.

Unspool them in ribbons and splice
the shredded places with golden
genomic scrap, and if we are lucky
they'll rise again, more substantial
than alchemy, more solid than ghosts.

Maybe a crooked wing, a halt
in the step, one blue eye where once
both were brown, but all the pieces,
new and old, must fit—no gaps, no holes,
no places we could slip through
like smoke and disappear inside
their baffled resurrected memory.

For who said the dead regret us, our messy
lusts, the bloody *coup d'etat,*
or even the unweeded garden,
the dog unfed on the porch?

We wander through bedrooms slamming
empty drawers, through kitchens
to bang the utensils,
all the while wailing *Tell us,*
tell us you love us!

We want what we want.
We search for it in anything we find:
a sock, a poem, a bone, a tooth,
a strand of DNA like spider's gossamer
twisted at the bottom
of a glass pipette.

Interstice

Dry as an August sun, cornstalks rustle and sigh
along the running path, a conversation
close enough to hear but not to comprehend.
Hooves of deer, paws of fox and field mice scuttle
in the fallen husks, invisible past three rows in.
They wait like breath inhaled and held
for me to pass along the road.

Slap of foot, flap of boot-sole, cadenced with drums
and dust, twang in my thigh and calf muscles
every time my sneakers hit the ground. I feel the rifle
rub against my shoulder with each step. The ghosts of soldiers,
marching west to Gettysburg, gaunt as smoke,
whispering behind me in the stalks of corn—

my sons, my grandsons—

Cosmic Background Radiation

for Liam Rector

In the crackling murk of static it makes
itself heard—not an echo but
the thing: creation's roar caroming
through the universe, the auditory everafter
of cosmic birth.

Do you know sound
and light can be distinguished
only by a length of wave,
the interpretive tools of an eye, an ear?

The big bang is no theory—it's real
as it sounds, the distant past impervious
to argument and reproach,
implacable as starlight.

And the heart? It receives
metaphor like a red antenna
and tries to decipher meaning in poetry,
tea-lights burning in fancy shoes,
a sad guitar.

At It Again

Those stacks of bullies
on my desk, those hardasses lined up
spine to smirking spine across the shelf:

What do you think you're doing,
you there, with the pen?
What could you have to say, you amateur,
that hasn't been said before
by people more eloquent than you?

Even the shabby ones, tossed in piles
on the floor, sneer and make faces.
If they had tongues, they'd stick them out.

I've heard it before, and it's probably true,
but I wanted to tell you
how the blue sky arcs above the hill
of Latimer's farm and the sun
sets behind the corn,
how the dharmic cows, swaying
as if gimbled, taste the back of your hand
with the tips of their tongues,
and sometimes
let you stroke their black noses, like wet leather,
with just one finger.

The Visitors

If they come, they come at dusk,
treeline shadows taking absolute form
at the bottom of the yard.

They sniff for danger, for illegal
day-old bagels and doughnuts,
yeasty heaps of contraband
stacked by the woodpile. Finding one
but not the other, they begin
to feast. They linger long enough
to eat their fill, then go invisible
in woods now darker than their fur.

Secret bears, secret bearers, they come
like smoke—then slip away like dreams
when daylight breaks, and you
can't remember anything
except you dreamed.

Good Luck All Day

They want to get rid of the penny,
underused, obsolete,
costs more to mint
than it spends.

But what then
of the old woman I saw this morning,
who pushed her walker to the curb,
saw copper bright as a sun
in the gutter, and bent to pick it up,
graceful as a girl?

Gardener's Sestina

Once again, this summer I've waited to plant
a garden until it's almost too late. I tend
to put things off, hanging fire until the last
possible second. But the seedlings will survive.
I'll be eating tomatoes in October. Field
mice will feast on the leavings in the cool rays

of November sun. I'd like to raise
rows of sweet corn, too, fat juicy watermelons, interplanted
with pole beans and morning glories. Imagine a field
of sunflowers and poppies, rampant but tended,
stretching from the kitchen window. We survive
on the periphery of nature, sometimes leave a last

corner of the yard half-wild to make ourselves feel wicked. Last
summer, I let one part of the garden raise
itself, a riot patch of weeds and volunteers, stalky survivors
of a mild winter and marauding rabbits. But each plant
felt like a reproach to my instinct to tend
and shape, and soon I flattened them to a field

of damp green mulch. Voles, snakes, field
mice, you name it, I reasoned, but at last
it was too much wildness, too close, too dangerous. We desire only tended
wilderness, nature under our thumbs. Daylilies raise
their sage crayola heads, nodding at the gardener's oxymoron. I planted
six bulbs last fall. Now there are twenty, surviving

and multiplying with biblical abandon. More survives
than we dream. We spend each spring ripping out fields
of crabgrass, puncture our hands on spiky nettles and dandelion plants
that won't die no matter what we pour on them. What lasts
is the wildness we can't tame, life's relentless yes raising
its voice above our neat rows and careful landscapes. Tend

the garden, cull and harvest and take what you will, tend
roses and roots until every growing thing you love survives,
flourishes in careful abundance. Rejoice in the starry rays
of a black-eyed Susan, the thick variegated field
of zinnia, cosmos, and yarrow, the last
tenacious clump of purple heather. But what you didn't plant

is there, too, waiting for the moment left untended,
waiting to invoke the wilderness that survives
at the garden's edge, warming under the same sun's rays.

Dream of Two Bears

"Whoever can sing the Song of the Bears has their lasting friendship."
—*The Haida People, British Columbia*

Heliotrope wafts its vanilla like a censer
to bless us, then tucks its purple flowers
beneath the rampant mint. So much is hidden, so much found

only in dreams, like a scent tracked through the leaf-fall
into the deepest forest where we are
the strangers with reflective eyes, our pupils black

pools of fear. We do not know the song
to keep us safe, we do not know the singers moving
between the trees, shaggy coat and daggered paw, prescient nose

exhaling mist and rich bass notes for us to follow
through the woods. The wild and fallow heart leaps up,
then goes still. Civilized, afraid, we cannot follow.

August Pastoral

The sheep does not mind much—
        not even the necessary attention to his wounds,
            ragged bite marks on his neck

from an old dog richoceted
        back to wildness
            by the archaic scent of prey.

The sheep and his fat brother are Zen masters
        of the barnyard, accepting
            rain and grass and first aid

with the same slow breath and placid stare.
        They swallow the world whole
            in a way we have forgotten,

who cannot see a rainbow arc
        across a summer sky without
            unprisming it into white light,

into something we think we understand.

The Forgiveness of Hummingbirds

A drought-strangled summer, too hot, too dry
to worry about the garden, water
restricted by law. The plants
wither and burn, and I do nothing.
No heart even to feed the birds—
the hummingbird nectar goes sour,
the feeder spout turning
black and flaky with mold.
Even the yellow jackets abandon it.

But one August morning, late summer guilt
finally moves me. In predawn murk
I turn an illicit hose on the whole yard
and dismantle the feeder, scrub and scour and boil
water and sugar for fresh nectar, even though I know
the hummingbirds have long since moved on.
The flowers hang their shriveled, sodden heads
as if praying for my undependable soul.
The morning turns brighter and hotter
while I stand barefoot in the damp grass, thinking
about responsibility and hundred-dollar fines.

Ordinary noises rise on the humid air,
cars revving, dogs barking, the slap
of a newspaper on pavement, then
out of nowhere, here he is—a male rubythroat
slurping the spillage around
the feeder's sticky cork, dipping
again and again into its dripping spout.
He hasn't read the books that say hummingbirds
are unforgiving, won't return
to feeder gone spoiled or empty.
His wings blur an iridescent green

as he drinks and drinks, hovering and backing and probing
with his long, elegant beak, his garnet red throat
quivering with every swallow—a little like forgiveness
to me watching in my pajamas,
the small blessing that comes
when you aren't looking, the improbable
gift you don't deserve.

Sister Parsnip

Consider the parsnip,
carrot's sturdy sister—
dependable, rooty, the underpinning
of winter stews and casseroles.
Not white, not yellow, she hangs out
with potatoes and onions, but can't
be topped with sour cream
or caramelized into French soup,
never deep-fried in batter for Super Bowl Sunday.
She plays third chair in the vegetable orchestra,
the single whole note beneath
a dinner's melody.

Her flamboyant sister gets all the dates—
no one ever blended a parsnip smoothie
or julienned her into arugula salad,
or baked her with nutmeg, topped her
with cream cheese, and brought her triumphant
to a birthday party. No one dips her
into ranch dressing and crunches her
at the health club. No cartoon bunny
sings songs to Sister Parsnip—
pale, a little hippy, she waits
for everyone, sensible
as thick-soled shoes.

Mea Non Culpa

If your balloon has burst,
        don't blame me.
I didn't sour the milk
        or poison the well

or forget to pay the cable bill.

It wasn't me who neglected
        to walk the dog
and left the wet clothes
        in the washing machine.

Don't look at me, I wasn't there

when you decided to tilt your chair
        backward until you fell
on your head. And those bad apples—
        you picked every one.

Who let the garden shears
        rust in the grass?
Who blew by the speed limit
        and wrecked the car?

Don't point a finger at me

if you can't pass the mirror
        without a shudder
after your lampshade dance.
        I wasn't playing that fiddle.

It ain't my fault, buster,
        if you're left standing there
with a scrap of ripped latex and string.
        Who pumped it up with hot air?

It was all you. Don't blame me for anything.

Revenge Poem

I'm putting you in my poem.
I'm putting you in my poem and there's nothing you can do about it
because it's my poem.

Because it's my poem I'm making you sit with no hat
on a city bench on a very sunny street
waiting for a bus that is very late.

You're sitting on the bench waiting for the bus
because something in the engine of your luxury hybrid SUV is broken
and is going to cost many dollars to fix.

The thing in your engine is broken because you weren't looking
where you were going and you crashed into an old lady's Buick
and demolished both your cars.

The old lady is the mother of a local Mafia big shot.
He's very very upset that you smashed up his mother's car.
His mother has whiplash. His brother is a lawyer.

The bus still hasn't come and you're starting to sweat.
Your pretty new ballet flats don't fit right, so you're getting a blister.
And then, because it's my poem, you also get a toothache.

So you sit sweating in the sun with a sore foot and a sore tooth
and start to ponder the old saying, "Be careful what you wish for."
Because you notice nobody wants to have lunch with you anymore

and you're spending your life at work putting out fires
and no one stops by your office to chat these days and now
you have no time to write. In fact, you're pretty sure you can't write anymore

because the last few things you scribbled down sounded like memos
and you just found out your book has been remaindered.
Also, at your most recent reading the audience consisted of two bookstore
          employees

and an old guy who thought it was Bass-Fishing Night and huffed off
when you started to read the new story about Love.
Speaking of Love, since this is my poem,

now your sweat is stinking a bit, and your tooth is throbbing
and your blister is bleeding all over your new ballet flat,
and you start to think about your husband,

who works even more than you and whom you only
see in passing on the way to bed. You start to count
the days since you last had sex and it's a really long time.

A really really long time. In fact, you lose count. You wonder for a second
if he's got a girlfriend, but he probably doesn't because he's a decent guy.
So maybe it is just you: you're not, as they say, as young as you used to be.

The truth is, though, you don't much want to have sex
because consolidating an empire takes a lot of energy.
Just ferreting out dissenters can suck up hours of your day.

Now you lean forward because you think you hear the bus
but it's the number 7, not the number 3, and when you lean back
you slide in the wet spot your dripping back made on the bench.

When you do, a splinter catches the fabric of your silk designer sundress
and pulls a tear about four inches long. Right around to the front
so your bra is clearly visible. It's a ratty old bra.

Between the sweat, the blister, and the tooth (screaming now),
your mascara has begun to run, and when a lady
passes by with her children, you look so alarming

she pulls them close and hurries them along. This hurts
your feelings, but this is my poem. Now I'm making you
remember the old children's book

about the turtle who piled all the other turtles up
and climbed atop them so he could be king of everything
he could see—which worked until the bottom turtle

got bored and walked out from under the pile.
You start wondering who at today's meeting
will be the first to walk out from under your pile.

Then the bus finally pulls up, belching exhaust,
but when you start to get on you realize you've only got
a twenty for a two-dollar ride. The driver gives you the hairy eyeball.

So you stick the twenty into the pay box (no change) and try to find an empty
        seat.
There aren't any. Also the air conditioning is broken.
So you squeeze your way back until you find a vacant strap.

This means, however, exposing your stinky armpit
to the masses. Those of the masses sitting directly
below your arm do not appreciate this. As you try to smile at them

to distract them from the odor and sight of your bra
you feel something in your mouth: it's your tooth, broken
off halfway. Did I mention it's a front tooth?

Also, the root's left behind so it still hurts.
When the bus reaches your stop, you squeeze out again
(the other passengers look relieved) into the open air

which isn't very open in this heat. As you walk
the three blocks home (no, let's make it six)
with your bloody ballet flat rubbing the blister more raw with every step,

you dig into your purse for a tissue, and the strap breaks, spilling
all your stuff on the sidewalk, including the mail
you picked up before leaving work

and shoved into your bag without reading. As you gather
all your belongings, you see that one of the envelopes
looks official. Because this is my poem,

you have to open it then and there.
It's from Human Resources, regretfully informing you
your dental insurance has been cancelled.

He Sent

A Google Poem

He sent me this
He sent me a strange message
He sent me a blank text
He sent me a happy birthday text
He sent me a drunk text
He sent me a charming card
He sent me angels
He sent me flowers
He sent me his son
He sent me a Boston terrier
He sent me his shirt buttons
He sent me a picture of his
He sent me running
He sent payment
He sent a white man to prison
He sent his daughters to study abroad
He sent them out two-by-two
He sent 160,000 demons
He sent them home sweating
He sent illegal gun magazines to governors
He sent suspicious bills to the Secret Service
He sent a man to the hospital
He sent me two Jehovah's Witnesses
He sent me the wrong item
He sent me his word—he does this for a living.

Relocation

If you find a house with a black snake and a ghost, buy it.
Lie down on the doorstep and don't move till it's yours.

Move in October, when the blue sky turns amethyst
and cornstalks wave like wizards' wands.

Build your first fire and feed it with salt.
Read your fortune in the colored flames,

a good one in a house like this!
The black snake is a blessing to keep

thieving varmints out. Listen to her sibilant song
and rejoice in her graceful slither.

Untether belief and turn the lamp down,
and you'll never be lonely.

The ghost will dance across your shadowed threshold,
good company in the dark winter.

The Feathered Man

for Abbas Ibn Firnas (810-887 A.D.)

"He flew faster than the phoenix in his flight
when he dressed his body in the feathers of a vulture."
                    —Mu'min Ibn Said, 9th century poet

Then he leapt off the cliff
onto the confidence of his own genius,
brash enough to hold him up
two hundred feet or so
as he swooped and dove
above the astonished faces
of the "trustworthy writers"
who witnessed his magical flight.

              No, no, not magic,
he knew, but invention and
the willingness to risk disaster,
which he almost met, forgetting
in the white heat of his Icaran vision
to make a tail to rudder him down,
so he crash-landed in a bloody heap
at the feet of the crowd.

Still, the teeth he spat out and
the torque in his spine were worth
all the pain. For the rest
of his life, as he hobbled by,
he heard the whispers floating
on the air of his wake:

It's true, they all saw it—
Like the birds, just like the birds,
he flew, he flew.

A Brief Exchange

But didn't you know to squander
is the worst kind of sin,
you beautiful sinner, you gaudy spender,
that a shower of sparks is not the sun?

Oh, I didn't squander, I slathered
a largesse of words on the ears of the world,
careless as a millionaire throwing dimes to the crowd—
and the dimes turned to light in their eager hands.

The Last Widow

Les Ventes, Normandy, France

Water your roots with hope, until hope passes over
like summer weather. The drought of loss
is a lifetime long, but the slender green stalk within
does not wither. The heart's eye
must see for itself. Go. You will find
a dead man, a dead plane, but also
memory and gratitude. We flinch and hunger
at the same time to hear of it,
although it is real as granite, as sand, as tears, as ashes.
Why do we flinch and hunger at the same time
to hear of it—a dead plane turned
to granite and sand; a dead man's ashes and tears?
Remember gratitude. Go, for the heart's eye
must see for itself. The slender green stalk within
does not wither, even though
the drought of loss is a lifetime long.
Hope will pass over like summer weather.
Your roots will be watered with it.

Hibernation, Ursa Major

Old she-bear, pent
in her rocky den,
gnaws a footpad
dry as dust,

solitary rakes in sticks
and scratches the scar
that marks a hunter's
mis-aimed lead.

Shaking the ice
off her frozen fur, she licks
the snow and huffs
out clouds of steam.

She glimpses the night
through a gap
in the rock, sees
her starry sister

whirl across the sky.
They watch each other
all the frigid season, nodding
across the distance.

The cubless months are long
but she'll wait out
dark days and the cold
morning rime.

Come spring,
she'll rise like heat
and blink into
the unfamiliar sun.

Come spring,
she'll sniff the air, nose
out what's been lost
by winter.

Author's Notes

"The Bears of Abruzzo"—The last population of Italy's Marsican bear, a subspecies of the Eurasian brown bear, has been reduced about thirty individuals. Protected by law, they live in the Abruzzo National Park between the mountains and the Adriatic Sea.

"Etymology"—The town of Portage, Alaska was destroyed in the 1964 earthquake and tsunami. One derelict house and many skeleton trees are still standing. *Timor mortis conturbat me*—"the fear of death confounds me"—is found in many medieval poems.

"Castrata"—The castrati were male singers surgically emasculated before puberty to maintain the purity of their voices. Although this practice dates back to ancient times, the heyday of the castrati was the 18th to early 19th centuries, concomitant with the rise of opera seria in western Europe. The best of these boy singers were given intensive training at renowned music schools in Italy and France. At maturity, the castrato had the crystalline clarity of a boy soprano; the range of an adult female soprano and an alto combined; and the power and resonance of an intact adult male tenor. Handel, Gluck, and Mozart all wrote leading operatic parts for castrati. The greatest castrato of all was Carlo Broschi Farinelli (1705-1782). Farinelli had a three-octave range, the ability to sing musical breath-phrases over a minute long, and a charismatic stage presence that won him a fanatical following. In 1737, he left the operatic stage to become chamber musician to King Philip V of Spain; Farinelli's singing was reported to be the only thing that could lift the king out of his lifelong debilitating depression.

"Cosmic Background Radiation" refers to the static heard on ordinary radio frequencies that is leftover sound of the Big Bang.

"Dream of Two Bears" is for John Eaton and for Hope.

"A Brief Exchange" is for Liam Rector.

"The Last Widow"—Lt. Billie Harris, a WW2 fighter pilot, went missing in action over Normandy in June 1944. His wife Peggy never received a definitive answer on his fate until 2005, when it was discovered that Lt. Harris had been shot down over the small town of Les Vents. He managed to maneuver his plane so he crashed outside the town, thereby saving the lives of the villagers. The villagers found his body, buried him, and still revere him as one of the heroes of the war. His remains were later relocated to the Allied Cemetery in Normandy; at this writing, Peggy Harris is last WW2 widow who still visits her husband's grave.

Laura Orem is the founder and director of the Women's Voices Mentorship Program for Writers. She is the author of the chapbook collection, *Castrata: a Conversation* (FLP 2014) and is a featured blogger at the Best American Poetry. Her work has been published in many venues, including *The Writer's Chronicle*, *DMQ*, *Zocalo Public Square*, *Nimrod*, and others. She holds an MFA from Bennington College and lives in Pennsylvania with her husband.